For the Teacher

This reproducible study guide to use in conjunction with a specific novel consists of instructional material for guided reading. Written in chapter-by-chapter format, the guide contains a synopsis, pre-reading activities, vocabulary and comprehension exercises, as well as extension activities to be used as follow-up to the novel.

NOVEL-TIES are either for whole class instruction using a single title or for group instruction where each group uses a different novel appropriate to its reading level. Depending upon the amount of time allotted to it in the classroom, each novel, with its guide and accompanying lessons, may be completed in two to four weeks.

The first step in using NOVEL-TIES is to distribute to each student a copy of the novel and a folder containing all of the duplicated worksheets. Begin instruction by selecting several pre-reading activities in order to set the stage for the reading ahead. Vocabulary exercises for each chapter always precede the reading so that new words will be reinforced in the context of the book. Use the questions on the chapter worksheets for class discussion or as written exercises.

The benefits of using NOVEL-TIES are numerous. Students read good literature in the original, rather than in abridged or edited form. The good reading habits formed by practice in focusing on interpretive comprehension and literary techniques will be transferred to the books students read independently. Passive readers become active, avid readers.

Novel-Ties® are printed on recycled paper.

SYNOPSIS

Things Fall Apart takes place at the beginning of the twentieth century in an Ibo village in Nigeria. Okonkwo has been one of the most highly respected men of the village for most of his adult life. But his three wives, numerous children, and many titles of honor have not made him a happy man. He is haunted by the memory of his father, a notorious failure in the eyes of his neighbors. Determined to live down the shame of a lazy and unsuccessful father, Okonkwo always seeks to improve his standing among his neighbors. One of his greatest worries is that his oldest son, Nwoye, does not show signs of wanting to follow in his father's footsteps.

With his children growing to adulthood, and his farm becoming more successful every year, Okonkwo is well on his way to the goal he has set for himself. Then, because of a single accident, the effects of all his efforts are destroyed. At a public ceremony for the upcoming wedding of his friend's son, Okonkwo fires a rifle in celebration and unwittingly kills a young villager; he and his family are forced to leave and spend the next seven years in the village where his mother was born.

While he is living in his mother's village, Okonkwo hears about disturbing changes in his home village. Christian missionaries and government officials from Great Britain have come to his village and have begun trying to change the traditional beliefs and customs of his people. After the British convert some villagers to Christianity, they introduce British laws and force them upon the villagers. By the time Okonkwo returns, the British have established a stronghold in the village, and most of the people are afraid to confront them. Okonkwo and five other men agree to talk with the British Commissioner, who promptly has them arrested. They are beaten and otherwise mistreated before they are released when the villagers pay a ransom. Okonkwo then calls a meeting of all the men in the village; his hope is that they will agree to fight the British and force them to leave. When a group of British policemen arrive to break up the meeting, Okonkwo retaliates by killing one of them. When the other villagers fail to join Okonkwo in the attack, he loses all hope and hangs himself, a shameful act that makes it impossible for fellow villagers to bury him with honor.

BACKGROUND INFORMATION

Nigeria

Nigeria, which is on the western coast of central Africa, has the largest population of any country on the continent. The population is divided into hundreds of ethnic groups, some of which can trace their ancestry to kingdoms that are centuries old. One of the largest ethnic groups is the Ibo, the group that is the subject of *Things Fall Apart*. During the seventeenth and eighteenth centuries, Nigerians came into contact with Europeans who went to Africa to establish trade relations or to take captives whom they sold as slaves. Several European countries struggled for control of Nigeria, until the British gained dominance about one hundred years ago. The novel is set during this period when the British outlawed the slave trade, introduced Christianity and European customs to Nigeria, and took steps to eliminate most of the traditional practices of the Nigerians. The British colonial government ruled Nigeria until 1960. Chinua Achebe wrote his novel in 1958, at a time when his country was preparing for independence, which came in 1960.

The Ibo

The Ibo (a name which is also spelled *Igbo*), the largest ethnic group in Nigeria, live mainly in the southeastern section of the country. They have traditionally lived off the land, mostly cultivating yams, cassava, and palm oil. Ibo society consisted of a series of villages which formed village groups, or confederations. It has long been their custom to elect leaders democratically and to choose their leaders from all age groups except the very youngest. The Ibo believe strongly in individualism, but not at the expense of the good of the group. Competition, especially in farming, is one of their highest ideals, but they also place a great deal of emphasis on cooperation within the group.

Although the Ibo value tradition highly, they have long been more willing to accept change than some neighboring clans. In fact, they are inclined to favor anything that improves the condition of either the individual or the group. Possibly for this reason, many Ibo were willing to accept the British officials and missionaries who brought them education, new farming techniques, and improved methods of trading.

PRE-READING ACTIVITIES

1. Preview the book by reading the title and the author's name and by looking at the illustration on the cover. What do you think the book will be about? Where and when does it take place? Have you read anything else by the same author?

2. Read the Background Information on Nigeria on page two of this study guide and do some additional research to learn about the history and culture of Nigeria. Find out about the state of the government and finances in Nigeria from the time it was granted independence by Great Britain in 1960 to the present time.

3. *Things Fall Apart* explores the significance of traditional beliefs and practices. What are some traditions that you follow? Are there any traditions that you think should be seriously questioned?

4. The main character in this novel is a man who is trying to live down his parent's bad reputation. Can you think of any contemporary public figures or celebrities who might have the same dilemma?

5. The central character in *Things Fall Apart* measured his success in life by how much respect he received from the people in his village and the surrounding villages. Do you believe that success should be measured by external criteria, internal criteria, or a combination of both?

6. Do you think parents should expect their children to follow in their footsteps? Should parents be prepared to see their children turn out to be different from themselves?

7. Because of his personality, the main character is driven to do things that may not be in his own best interests. Can you think of any other fictional characters or famous people who might have the same failing?

8. The modern era is characterized as a time of rapid change. What kinds of changes should people be prepared for during their lifetimes? What kinds of changes do you think people should resist as much as they can?

9. Chinua Achebe wrote *Things Fall Apart* in 1958 to dramatize what happened when the culture of one people came into conflict with the culture of another. He believed that this usually resulted in the combination of their worst elements. What are some examples of how Americans have taken elements from other cultures? What are some examples of how other people have taken elements of American culture? Discuss how some of these exchanges were positive and others were negative.

10. Read the excerpt from the William Butler Yeats poem "The Second Coming" that appears opposite the title page. With a partner, discuss the possible meaning of these lines. Obtain a copy of the entire poem to see if it reinforces or contradicts your interpretation of the excerpt. As you read the book, try to determine why the author chose these lines to introduce the book.

CHAPTERS 1 – 3

Vocabulary: Draw a line from each word on the left to its definition on the right. Then use the numbered words to answer the questions below.

1. wily		a.	lacking foresight; careless
2. improvident		b.	strange; eerie
3. haggard		c.	deceptive; tricky
4. dense		d.	sad
5. impending		e.	exhausted; worn out
6. intricate		f.	complicated
7. plaintive		g.	very thick
8. uncanny		h.	threatening; about to happen

. . . .

1. Which word might describe a song or poem that makes listeners want to cry?

   _____

2. Which word might describe jungle foliage that is hard to walk through?

   _____

3. Which word might describe a real estate broker who does not reveal any of the problems in a house that is being sold? _____

4. Which word might be used in a weather report of a storm that is only hours away?

   _____

5. Which word might describe an unbelievable coincidence? _____

6. Which word might describe someone who never saved money for retirement?

   _____

7. Which word might describe someone who has just been rescued after wandering in the desert for three weeks? _____

8. Which word might describe the design of a maze? _____

Chapters 1 – 3 (cont.)

Questions:

1. Why was "throwing Amalinze the Cat" such an important event during Okonkwo's teenage years? Why do you think the author used this event to introduce the protagonist of this novel?

2. Why was Unoka considered a failure in Ibo society?

3. What motivated Okonkwo to succeed in life? Was he successful? How did his driven personality affect his family?

4. What did the Ibo beliefs about darkness and snakes reveal about the Ibo attitude toward the world?

5. Why was the village of Umuofia feared and respected by its neighbors?

6. How did Ikemefuna come to live in Okonkwo's home?

7. Why did Okonkwo ask Nwakibie for yam seeds? Why did Nwakibie agree to help him?

8. How did Okonkwo regard his difficult first year of farming? What did this suggest about his future?

Questions for Discussion:

1. Do you think Unoka was judged fairly by his society?

2. Do you think Okonkwo was justified in wanting to win the respect of his neighbors?

Literary Devices:

I. *Simile*—A simile is a figure of speech in which a comparison of two unlike objects is made using the words "like" or "as." For example:

Okonkwo's fame had grown like a bush-fire in the harmattan.

What is being compared?

_____

What does this reveal about Okonkwo?

_____

_____

Chapters 1 – 3 (cont.)

II. *Flashback*—A flashback refers to the return to an earlier time in a story for the purpose of clarifying something in the present. Why do you think the author introduced Okonkwo as an adult and then flashed back to an earlier time, focusing on Okonkwo's father?

_____

_____

_____

Social Studies Connection:

Review Chapters One through Three to determine what represents wealth and prosperity in rural Ibo society. What might a wealthly Ibo villager possess? How does this compare with signs of wealth in your own society?

Writing Activities:

1. Write a conversation that might have taken place between Okonkwo and his father shortly before the old man died.

2. Write about a time when you or someone you know was humiliated by the words or deeds of another family member.

CHAPTERS 4 – 6

Vocabulary: Use the context to determine the meaning of the underlined word in each of the following sentences. Then use a dictionary to find the exact meaning of the word.

1. The fund-raising sale was successful because of the <u>industry</u> of the students.

    Your definition_____

    Dictionary definition _____

2. My father was such a <u>benevolent</u> person that he gave all of his money away to charitable causes before he died.

    Your definition_____

    Dictionary definition _____

3. The coach wanted to <u>minimize</u> the risk of injury to all the players.

    Your definition_____

    Dictionary definition _____

4. The rules for that contest are so <u>exacting</u> that no one could possibly win.

    Your definition_____

    Dictionary definition _____

5. The child told a <u>poignant</u> story that had everyone close to tears.

    Your definition_____

    Dictionary definition _____

6. My sister is a screenwriter, but her <u>ultimate</u> goal is to become a movie director.

    Your definition_____

    Dictionary definition _____

7. The governor took a <u>tentative</u> step toward raising taxes, but then backed away.

    Your definition_____

    Dictionary definition _____

8. All her friends tried to <u>console</u> her when she learned she didn't get the scholarship.

    Your definition_____

    Dictionary definition _____

Chapters 4 – 6 (cont.)

9. If you are <u>persistent</u> in your studies, your grades are likely to improve.

   Your definition_____

   Dictionary definition _____

10. After the last play of the game, the crowd <u>surged</u> toward the exits.

   Your definition_____

   Dictionary definition _____

Questions:

1. Why did an old man remind Okonkwo that his palm-kernels were cracked by a benevolent spirit? Why did Okonkwo feel that his success was not due to luck?

2. How did Okonkwo feel about Ikemefuna? Why was he unable to express his feelings to the boy?

3. Why did the priest Ezeani consider Okonkwo's transgression to be a greater sin than that of his second wife?

4. What kept Okonkwo from enjoying the New Yam Festival?

5. Why did Ekwefi, Okonkwo's second wife, enjoy the wrestling matches more than any other activity during the New Yam Festival?

6. Why did Okonkwo have a special fondness for his daughter Ezinma?

Questions for Discussion:

1. What was the real and symbolic significance of yams in Ibo culture? Why do you think the New Year celebration centered around the planting of the yams?

2. How would you characterize Okonkwo's relationship with his wife and children? Why do you think his behavior was tolerated by Ibo society?

3. What do you think the wrestling match revealed about the values of the people of the village?

Literary Devices:

I. *Foreshadowing*—Foreshadowing in literature refers to clues that suggest what will happen later in a story. What do you think the incident of Okonkwo shooting at his second wife might foreshadow?

   _____

   _____

Chapters 4 – 6 (cont.)

II. *Simile*—What is being compared in the following similes?

> The air, which had been stretched taut with excitement, relaxed again. It was as if water had been poured on the tightened skin of a drum.

_____

> The drummers took up their sticks and the air shivered and grew tense like a tightened bow.

_____

How do these figures of speech enhance the meanings of the statements?

_____

_____

Social Studies Connection:

What has this book revealed about the role of women in traditional Ibo society? Do some research to learn about the role of women in contemporary Nigeria.

Science Connection:

Do some research to learn about the climate and geography of Nigeria. When is the rainy season? What crops are grown? What part of the country has an agricultural economy?

Writing Activity:

Write about any of the following aspects of traditional Ibo society using information you have learned from the book.

- Relationships between parents and children
- Relationships between husband and wives
- Practice of polygamy
- Division of labor
- Role of religion

CHAPTERS 7 – 9

Vocabulary: Analogies are equations in which the first pair of words has the same relationship as the second pair of words. For example: ENORMOUS is to HUGE as ENTERTAIN is to AMUSE. Both pairs or words are synonyms. Choose the best word from the Word Box to complete each of the analogies below.

WORD BOX				
agility	devoid	emissary	prosperous	sparse
audacity	elude	malevolence	restrain	specious

1. GLOOMY is to CHEERFUL as _____ is to FULL.

2. ENCLOSE is to CONTAINER as _____ is to LEASH.

3. ATHLETE is to _____ a SCHOLAR is to INTELLIGENCE.

4. GENEROSITY so to GOOD as _____ is to EVIL.

5. GENUINE is to REAL as _____ is to FAKE.

6. SHY is to TIMIDITY as BOLD is to _____.

7. CREATE is to INVENT as _____ is to ESCAPE.

8. _____ is to SUCCESS as SICK is to ILLNESS.

9. _____ is to ERRAND as EXPLORER is to EXPEDITION.

10. ABUNDANT is to EXCESS as _____ is to SHORTAGE.

Questions:

1. How had Ikemefuna's arrival in Okonkwo's household affected Nwoye? Why did this please Okonkwo?

2. What was the difference between the tales Okonkwo told to the boys and those Nwoye's mother told to the younger children?

3. Why were the villagers delighted when locusts descended?

4. Why did Okonkwo ignore Ezeudu's advice not to take part in the execution of Ikemefuna?

5. How did Nwoye react to the death of Ikemefuna? How did Okonkwo react? Why do you think he reacted this way?

Chapters 7 – 9 (cont.)

6. What did Obierika and Okonkwo's remarks about white men and the customs in other places reveal about them and their tribe?

7. Why did Ekwefi have such a close relationship with her daughter Ezinma?

Questions for Discussion:

1. What was the significance of the folk tales Okonkwo told the boys? What was the significance of the tales Nwoye's mother told to the younger children? Are there any legends or tales that you have heard, read, or seen on film? What values or messages did they convey?

2. Do you think Okonkwo was justified in treating his sons and his wives so sternly?

3. Do you think Okonkwo should have participated in Ikemefuna's killing, or do you agree with Obierika that he should not have participated? Might Okonkwo have stopped the killing?

Literary Element: Setting

Setting refers to the time and place a story occurs. Reread the section of Chapter Seven when Ikemefuna is being led through the forest for his execution. How did the description of the setting contrast with and also reinforce the action that took place?

_____

_____

_____

Science Connection:

Traditional Ibo culture depended upon folk wisdom and medicine men to cure illness. Do some research on folk medicine to learn about traditional remedies that are entering the mainstream of Western medicine. Conduct a survey of your classmates to learn about the folk remedies used by their families. What modern medical practice is similar to the one Okonkwo used to treat his daughter Ezinma?

Writing Activity:

Write about a time when you, like Okonkwo, were torn between what society expected of you and what your emotions dictated. Tell whether you took any action and what was the result.

CHAPTERS 10 – 13

Vocabulary: Synonyms are words with similar meanings. Draw a line from each word in column A to its synonym in column B. Then use the words in column A to fill in the blanks in the sentences below.

	A		B
1.	delirious	a.	obscure
2.	esoteric	b.	infamous
3.	luxuriant	c.	piercing
4.	notorious	d.	raving
5.	prominent	e.	quivering
6.	shrill	f.	conspicuous
7.	sullen	g.	abundant
8.	tremulous	h.	glum

. . . .

1. The _____ sound of the siren pierced the air.

2. The _____ aims of the leaders remained a mystery to the press and the residents of the surrounding town.

3. The mayor was removed from office once she became _____ for giving city jobs to her friends and relatives.

4. After days of rain, the garden became so _____ that it was impossible to walk down the path.

5. Perhaps a vacation in the country will put an end to your _____ mood.

6. One of the most _____ features of Paris is the Eiffel Tower.

7. The old man spoke in a(n) _____ voice.

8. High fever might cause a patient to become _____.

Questions:

1. How were legal matters handled in Okonkwo's village? What did the disposition of Mgbafo's case indicate about the status of women?

2. What did Ekwefi's night-long walk reveal about her? Why do you think Okonkwo followed behind her?

Chapters 10 – 13 (cont.)

3. How were the villagers informed that someone died? What evidence showed that it was a warrior's funeral?

4. Why was Okonkwo exiled from his village?

Questions for Discussion:

1. Why do you think the Ibo hearing was preceded by religious ceremony and decisions were made by people impersonating ancestral spirits?

2. What human qualities were valued and which ones were criticized in the tale told by Ekwefi?

3. What aspects of life were regulated by custom in Okonkwo's village? What aspects of life offered people free choice? Do you think life was over-regulated or that life was pleasant because it was so well-ordered?

4. Do you think Okonkwo's family should have been forced to share Okonkwo's punishment?

5. Why do you think the author did not name the slain youth?

Literary Device: Point of View

Point of view refers to the voice telling the story. It could be third person narrative in which the author tells the story, or first person narrative in which one of the characters tells the story. In this third person narrative, find examples of the following:

• narrator who knows the thoughts of several characters

_____

_____

• narrator who seems to be in the mind of Okonkwo

_____

_____

• narrator who seems to be in the mind of some other character

_____

_____

Chapters 10 – 13 (cont.)

Compare and Contrast:

Use a Venn diagram, such as the one below, to compare rituals of birth, marriage, or death in an Ibo village to those in your own culture. List similarities in the overlapping part of the circles.

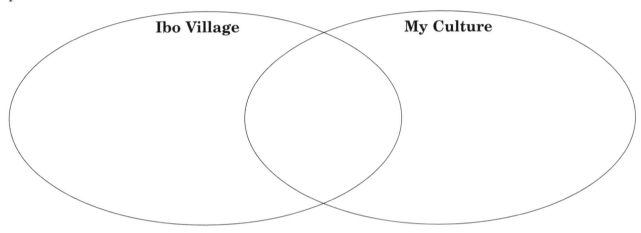

Ibo Village   My Culture

Cooperative Learning Activity:

Work with a cooperative learning group to complete a chart such as the one below and then discuss the questions that follow.

Basic values in an Ibo village	Basic values in Western society

1. Is it possible for an individual to support the value system of a society but selectively exclude some of its tenets?

2. If people allow any of a society's values to come into question, is the entire society vulnerable?

3. Can Okonkwo remain true to the value system of his tribe and yet dispute the punishment for inadvertent killing?

Writing Activity:

Imagine that you are Nwoye or Ezinma and write a journal entry describing your thoughts and feelings on the day of your family's exile.

CHAPTERS 14 – 19

Vocabulary: Use the context to determine the meaning of the underlined word in each of the following sentences. Then draw a line from each word to its definition below.

- If you haven't completed the <u>requisite</u> documents, the department will not issue a passport.

- Black clouds overhead were an <u>ominous</u> sign of storms approaching our area.

- The ants <u>persevered</u> until they stripped the entire plant of all its green leaves.

- Everyone was certain the convicted criminal would receive a long jail term for committing a <u>despicable</u> crime.

- She had a <u>perplexed</u> expression on her face as she tried to read the map after it had been torn.

- The heavy bombing almost <u>annihilated</u> the city.

- After revealing embarrassing secrets in his books, the author was <u>ostracized</u> by his entire family.

- Frost on the ground in October is a <u>harbinger</u> of a cold winter ahead.

. . . .

1. requisite
2. ominous
3. persevered
4. despicable
5. perplexed
6. annihilated
7. ostracized
8. harbinger

a. maintained a purpose in spite of difficulties
b. completely destroyed
c. bewildered; puzzled
d. required or necessary
e. banished; shunned
f. anything that foreshadows a future event
g. threatening evil or harm
h. vile; detestable

Questions:

1. How did Uchendu and his mother's other kinsmen try to make Okonkwo's banishment to their village as comfortable as possible?

2. Why was Okonkwo's life on his new farm compared to "learning to become left-handed in old age"?

3. What news did Obierika bring to Okonkwo during his second year of exile? What did this event reveal about the Ibo and their world?

Chapters 14 – 19 (cont.)

4. What disturbing news did Obierika bring to Okonkwo during his fourth year of exile? Why did this news disturb Okonkwo?

5. What feature of Christianity was especially appealing to Okonkwo's son Nwoye? How was this appeal consistent with Nwoye's earlier behavior? How did Okonkwo's reaction confirm Nwoye's decision to accept Christianity?

6. Why did the village elders offer land to the missionaries to build a church? How did this plan backfire?

7. How did the acceptance of Ibo outcasts strengthen the Christian church in Mbanta?

8. How did Okonkwo mark the occasion of his leaving Mbanta? Why did he do this? What message did he impart to the men of his clan?

Questions for Discussion:

1. Why do you think banishment might have been worse for Okonkwo than for most other members of his village?

2. Do you think it was wrong for the villagers of Abame to kill the white man who rode a bicycle into their village? Did the villagers deserve their punishment?

3. Do you think it was appropriate for Christian missionaries to evangelize in Ibo villages?

Literary Style:

Why do you think the changes in village life were presented second-hand, rather than directly witnessed by Okonkwo, the main character in the book? What did the time frame within which the events of change occurred reveal about the nature of this change?

Writing Activities:

1. Write about a time when you or someone you know could have succumbed to self-pity. Describe the cause of this feeling and tell whether it undermined its object.

2. Write about an event or series of events that changed your way of life. Indicate the source of this change and tell whether the change was reversible.

CHAPTERS 20 – 25

Vocabulary: Antonyms are words with opposite meanings. Draw a line from each word in column A to its antonym in column B. Then use the words in column A to complete the sentences below.

A		B	
1.	esteem	a.	necessary
2.	zeal	b.	disinterest
3.	expedient	c.	undecided
4.	desolate	d.	disrespect
5.	discordant	e.	harmonious
6.	superfluous	f.	cheerful
7.	resolute	g.	disadvantageous

. . . .

1. No matter how hard we argued, she was absolutely _____ in her decision to go to a private college.

2. His _____ for the game of chess was evident in the number of hours he practiced and the many books he read on the subject.

3. Since I have planned the party completely, any food you bring would be _____.

4. The award they gave her proved that they held her work in high _____.

5. The city was a(n) _____ sight after its war-weary citizens left.

6. The _____ sounds of untuned violins made my head ache.

7. Politicians always find it more _____ to lower taxes in an election year than at any other time.

Questions:

1. How was Okonkwo's return home different from what he expected?

2. What surprised Okonkwo about the people who had joined the Christian church?

3. According to Obierika, why couldn't the Ibo regain control over Abame and the other villages?

Chapters 20 – 25 (cont.)

4. Why was Mr. Brown held in greater regard by the Ibo than his successor, Mr. Smith?

5. What evidence showed that the unmasking of the *egwugwu* was very important to the villagers of Abame?

6. What did the manner of the arrest of the six villagers and their subsequent treatment reveal about the British officials?

7. How did Okonkwo's use of force as an attempt to bring about a solution to the villager's problems with the British show that he was out of touch with the changes that had taken place during his exile?

Questions for Discussion:

1. In what ways was Okonkwo still an exile even after he returned to his village?

2. Referring to the long conversation between Mr. Brown and Akunna, what are some of the similarities and differences between the Ibo faith and Christianity?

3. Do you think the Ibo villagers might have reached an agreement with the British and still have retained their traditional ways?

4. What are the several ways that Okonkwo's suicide could be seen as a tragedy? Do you think his death was inevitable?

Literary Devices:

I. *Symbolism*—A symbol in literature is an object, an event, or a character that represents an idea or a set of ideas. What did the Enoch's unmasking of the *egwugwu* symbolize?

_____

What did Okonkwo's death symbolize?

_____

II. *Simile*—What is being compared in the following simile:

> Umofia was like a startled animal with ears erect, sniffing the silent, ominous air and not knowing which way to run.

_____

Why is this an apt comparison?

_____

_____

Chapters 20 – 25 (cont.)

III. *Irony*—Irony refers to the conflict between appearance and reality. What was ironic about the title of the book the District Commissioner intended to write?

_____

_____

_____

_____

Literary Element: Characterization

Okonkwo was presented as a character of great complexity. How was his dominant characteristic of pride both a positive and negative force in his life?

_____

_____

_____

_____

Writing Activity:

Write two obituaries for Okonkwo in which you recount the events of his life. The first obituary should be from the point of view of an Ibo villager and the second should be from the point of view of a British government official.

CLOZE ACTIVITY

The following passage has been taken from Chapter Two of the novel. Read it through completely and then fill in each blank with a word that makes sense. Afterwards, you may compare your language with that of the author.

Okonkwo ruled his household with a heavy hand. His wives, especially the youngest, lived in _____ [1] fear of his fiery temper, and so _____ [2] his little children. Perhaps down in his _____ [3] Okonkwo was not a cruel man. But his _____ [4] life was dominated by fear, the fear _____ [5] failure and of weakness. It was deeper _____ [6] more intimate than the fear of evil _____ [7] capricious gods and of magic, the fear _____ [8] the forest, and of the forces of _____, [9] malevolent, red in tooth and claw. Okonkwo's _____ [10] was greater than these. It was not _____ [11] but lay deep within himself. It was _____ [12] fear of himself, lest he should be _____ [13] to resemble his father. Even as a _____ [14] boy he had resented his father's failure _____ [15] weakness, and even now he still remembered _____ [16] he had suffered when a playmate had _____ [17] him that his father was *agbala*. That _____ [18] how Okonkwo first came to know that _____ [19] was not only another name for a _____, [20] it could also mean a man who _____ [21] taken no title. And so Okonkwo was _____ [22] by one passion—to hate everything that _____ [23] father Unoka had loved. One of those _____ [24] was gentleness and another was idleness.

During _____ [25] planting season Okonkwo worked daily on his _____ [26] from cock-crow until the chickens went to _____. [27] He was a very strong man and _____ [28] felt fatigue. But his wives and young _____ [29] were not as strong, and so they _____. [3] But they dared not complain openly. Okonkwo's _____ [31] son, Nwoye, was then twelve years old _____ [32] was already causing his father great anxiety _____ [33] his incipient laziness. At any rate, that _____ [34] how it looked to his father, and _____ [35] sought to correct him by constant nagging _____ [36] beating. And so Nwoye was developing into a sad-faced youth.

POST-READING ACTIVITIES

1. Return to the excerpt from William Butler Yeats' poem "The Second Coming" that appears at the beginning of the book. Why do you now think Achebe alluded to this poem?

2. In a classical Greek tragedy, the hero falls due to one significant flaw. If Okonkwo were to be viewed as a classical hero, what might be seen as his tragic flaw? Trace how this shortcoming led to his personal tragedy.

3. Okonkwo blames the end of his traditional culture on the arrival of the British. There are several points in the novel, however, before the British arrive, when several characters show doubts, or even outright rejection, of some Ibo beliefs and practices. Identify some of these incidents and decide whether you think they indicated that Ibo civilization might have been ready to change even if the British had not colonized Nigeria.

4. Do some research to learn about Nigeria in the years after the time covered in this novel. Read about Nigeria and the Ibo from approximately 1900 to the present. Look at newspapers and international news magazines to find current articles about Nigeria. What is their government? Are there any conflicts in Nigeria at this time?

5. How might Okonkwo's village and Okonkwo's personal experiences be seen as a microcosm of the entire African continent as it was affected by colonialism? What evidence was there that the colonials were sowing the seeds of their own ultimate destruction?

6. One of the marks of a literary classic is that its story rises above its setting and appeals to people from different places and different cultures. Think about why many people call *Things Fall Apart* a classic. In what ways does it reach beyond its setting? What are its universal themes? How effectively do you think it deals with these themes?

SUGGESTIONS FOR FURTHER READING

* Borland, Hal. *When the Legends Die*. Random House.

  Cooper, James Fenimore. *The Last of the Mohicans*. Random House.

* Craven, Margaret. *I Heard the Owl Call My Name*. Random House.

  Dinesen, Isaak. *Out of Africa*. Random House.

* George, Jean Craighead. *Julie of the Wolves*. HarperCollins.

  Gordimer, Nadine. *July's People*. Penguin.

* Gordon, Sheila. *Waiting for the Rain*. Random House.

  Markham, Beryl. *The Splendid Outcast*. Random House.

* O'Dell, Scott. *Sing Down the Moon*. Random House.

* Orwell, George. *1984*. New American Library.

  Paton, Alan. *Cry, the Beloved Country*. Scribner's.

  _____. *Too Late the Phalarope*. Scribner's.

* Richter, Conrad. *The Light in the Forest*. Random House.

  Soyinka, Wole. *Ake: The Years of Childhood* (an autobiography). Random House.

* Steinbeck, John. *The Pearl*. Penguin.

  Tutuola, Amos. *My Life in the Bush of Ghosts*. Grove/Atlantic.

Some Other Books by Chinua Achebe

Anthills of the Savannah. Random House.

Arrow of God. Random House.

Chike and the River. Cambridge University Press.

Girls at War and Other Stories. Random House.

Home and Exile. Random House.

How the Leopard Got His Claws. The Third Press.

A Man of the People. Random House.

No Longer at Ease. Random House.

Sister of My Heart. Random House.

* NOVEL-TIES Study Guide are available for these titles.

ANSWER KEY

Chapters 1–3

Vocabulary: 1. c 2. a 3. e 4. g 5. h 6. f 7. d 8. b; 1. plaintive 2. dense 3. wily 4. impending 5. uncanny 6. improvident 7. haggard 8. intricate

Questions: 1. "Throwing Amalinze" was a way for Okonkwo to gain the respect of the villagers. Answers to the second part of the question will vary, but may include the idea that the recounting of this wrestling match immediately established Okonkwo's physical strength and competitive spirit. 2. Unoka was considered a failure because he was poor, had only one wife, owed a great deal of money, had taken no title, was not interested in war, and preferred playing his flute to working the land. 3. Okonkwo was motivated to succeed in order to overcome the shame his father cast on the family. According to Ibo standards, Okonkwo had succeeded in all ways. Because Okonkwo feared any comparison with his father, he showed no gentleness or sensitivity. Thus, he ruled his household harshly. 4. Fear of darkness and snakes revealed a fear of the unknown and a fear of surprising dangers. 5. Umuofia was feared and respected because of its strength in war tempered by fairness. It was also noted for its powerful magic and medicine men. 6. The clan, who had acquired Ikemefuna as compensation instead of war, had asked Okonkwo to house him until they decided his fate. 7. Okonkwo asked Nwakibie for yam seeds because he was a prosperous man who could help Okonkwo get a start in life. Nwakibie agreed to assist Okonkwo after turning down other village youth because he recognized Okonkwo's strength and drive. 8. Okonkwo regarded his first difficult year as a sign that he could survive because he was a fighter. His optimism despite great odds suggested a successful future.

Chapters 4 – 6

Vocabulary: 1. industry–hard work 2. benevolent–kindly 3. minimize–reduce to the smallest amount 4. exacting–demanding 5. poignant–touching; sad 6. ultimate–final 7. tentative–hesitant; experimental 8. console–comfort 9. persistent–steadfast; tenacious 10. surged–moved suddenly and powerfully

Questions: 1. An old man, who was critical of Okonkwo's lack of humility, told him that his success was due to the assistance of a benevolent spirit. Okonkwo knew, however, that he had worked hard and made his own success. 2. Okonkwo became very fond of Ikemefuna, thinking of him as a son. Okonkwo did not show his feelings because he was afraid that would reveal a sensitivity that would be embarrassing. 3. Ezeani considered Okonkwo's sin of beating his wife during the week of peace prior to the planting of crops to be the ultimate sin because angry gods might punish the entire community by reducing the food supply. 4. Okonkwo could not enjoy feasts or the time spent in preparation beforehand because he resented taking time away from work. 5. Ekwefi probably felt nostalgic about the wrestling matches because they reminded her of the young Okonkwo with whom she had fallen in love and for whom she had left her husband and village. 6. Okonkwo had a special fondness for Ezinma because she was very bright and reminded him of Ekwefi when she was young and the most beautiful woman in the village.

Chapters 7 – 9

Vocabulary: 1. devoid 2. restrain 3. agility 4. malevolence 5. specious 6. audacity 7. elude 8. prosperous 9. emissary 10. sparse

Questions: 1. Since Ikemefuna's arrival, Nwoye had become more motivated in his work and had seemed to mature according to Ibo standards. Okonkwo was pleased because he had worried that his son Nwoye might have inherited his grandfather's laziness. 2. Okonkwo told the boys tales of violence and bloodshed, while Nwoye's mother told the young children "pourquoi" tales—those that used myth to explain phenomena of nature. 3. The villagers were delighted by the arrival of the locusts because they were a novelty as well as a source of food. 4. Okonkwo ignored Ezeudu's advice because he did not want to appear weak in the villagers' eyes. 5. Nwoye was devastated by Ikemefuna's death. He looked upon his father, one of Nwoye's executioners, as though he were an evil spirit. Okonkwo had trouble eating and sleeping after Ikemefuna's death. He seemed physically weak and mentally anguished. Answers to the last part of the question will vary, but may include the idea that he felt guilty about taking part in the killing of someone who had been like a son to him. 6. Okonkwo and Obierika's remarks indicated that they and other villagers knew that Europeans were colonizing more and more in Africa. 7. Ekwefi was particularly devoted to Ezinma because nine of her other children had died in infancy. Although Ezinma lived, she had periods of illness that made her life seem even more precious.

Chapters 10 – 13

Vocabulary: 1. d 2. a 3. g 4. b 5. f 6. c 7. h 8. e; 1. shrill 2. esoteric 3. notorious 4. luxuriant 5. sullen 6. prominent 7. tremulous 8. delirious

Questions: 1. Matters requiring legal justice were settled at a hearing before the entire village and decided

upon by nine important village elders masquerading as ancestral spirits. At the hearing each side could present its case and pertinent witnesses. The nine men would confer and pronounce their decision. Although Mgbafo's family seemed to make a good case against her husband for his brutality, he was given a small punishment and granted the return of his wife. This suggested that women were inconsequential. The next case, having to do with land rights, was considered more important. 2. Ekwefi's night-long walk revealed her love and dedication to her daughter. It also revealed that she was willing to risk disturbing the goddess. Answers to the second part of the question will vary, but may include the idea that Okonkwo was equally devoted to his daughter Ezinma. 3. A specific drumbeat informed the villagers that a death had occurred. The wild dancing and raffia costumes indicated that it was a warrior's funeral. 4. Okonkwo was exiled from his village because he had upset the established order by inadvertently killing a young boy at the funeral ceremony.

Chapters 14 – 19
Vocabulary: 1. d 2. g 3. a 4. h 5. c 6. b 7. e 8. f

Questions: 1. To make Okonkwo's banishment as comfortable as possible, his kinsmen gave him land, helped him to build a new compound, and gave him sufficient seed yams to start a new farm. Also, Uchendu explained to Okonkwo that he should take consolation from being in his mother's homeland and make certain that his family did not become weighed down with his disappointment. 2. Although Okonkwo had his family around him and was given land to farm, he had lost his motivation. It was as difficult and awkward for him to begin anew as it would be for someone to learn to write in a new way. 3. During his second year in exile, Obierika reported that an entire Ibo village had been obliterated by white men in retaliation for their killing of a man who had entered the village on a bicycle. This event revealed that the Ibo were ignorant of Europeans and knew nothing about their growing number in Africa. 4. During his fourth year in exile, Obierika told how the missionaries and government officials from England had changed village life. Okonkwo was disturbed because he saw this as a threat to the traditional Ibo way of life and its value system. 5. Nwoye especially liked the poetic stories at the heart of Christian beliefs; this was consistent with the pleasure he took in the stories his mother used to tell him. Okonkwo's reaction of a physical threat to his son confirmed Nwoye's decision to disobey his father and pursue the Christian faith. 6. Rather than turn them down and risk a confrontation, the village elders offered the Christian missionaries land that they believed was inhabited by evil spirits. When nothing evil happened to the missionaries, Ibo belief was undermined and the Christian missionaries gained new converts. 7. By accepting outcasts, the church gained dedicated adherents. Also, when others who were more tentative saw that no harm came to them in the presence of outcasts, they became stronger adherents. 8. Okonkwo gave a huge feast for the villagers who had been his hosts for seven years because he wanted to share his prosperity with them. Okonkwo reminded the younger generation of Mbanta about the importance of maintaining strong links of kinship and the traditional hierarchy.

Chapters 20 – 25
Vocabulary: 1. d 2. b 3. g 4. f 5. e 6. a 7. c; 1. resolute 2. zeal 3. superfluous 4. esteem 5. desolate 6. discordant 7. expedient

Questions: 1. Okonkwo expected to be welcomed as a great man; instead, most people barely acknowledged his return. 2. Okonkwo was surprised that the church had won converts not only among the clan's outcasts, but also among its well-respected people. 3. Because the British government officials had been preceded by the missionaries, and because many Ibo had joined the missionaries, it would be impossible for the Ibo to use violent means against the white men without hurting their own people. 4. Mr. Brown was respected because he was reasonable, he respected the beliefs and traditions of the Ibo, and he tried to find a compromise between their beliefs and his own. Mr. Smith had a hostile attitude toward non-Christians, and he believed that there was only one right way—Christian orthodoxy. For him, there was no compromise or understanding of tradition. 5. The importance of the unmasking was shown by the fact that it provoked a gathering of all the *egwugwu* from Abame and all the neighboring villages. It was also the one act that was serious enough to provoke a confrontation between the Ibo and the British missionaries in which the Ibo burned down the church in retaliation for the unmasking. 6. Although the British pretended to call the meeting for purposes of friendship and understanding, they really meant to overpower and arrest the six village representatives. This revealed that the British were more concerned with power than they were with future good relations. This was confirmed by the humiliating treatment that the six men received in jail. 7. Okonkwo thought he was protecting the villagers' beliefs when he was actually defending an ideal that most of them had relinquished.